MAKING
MISSIONARY
DISCIPLES

MAKING MISSIONARY DISCIPLES

HOW TO LIVE *the* METHOD

MODELED BY *the* MASTER

Published in the United States by FOCUS, the Fellowship of Catholic
University Students, Genesee, Colorado. www.focus.org

FOCUS is a trademark of the Fellowship of Catholic University Students.

Nihil Obstat:	David N. Uebbing, B.A., M.A.
	Censor Librorum
Imprimatur:	+Most Reverend Samuel J. Aquila, S.T.L.
	Archbishop of Denver
	Denver, Colorado, USA
	March 21, 2018

The Nihil Obstat and Imprimatur are official declarations that a book or
pamphlet is free of doctrinal or moral error. No implication is contained
therein that those who have granted the Nihil Obstat or Imprimatur
agree with the content, opinions, or statements expressed.

ISBN-13: 978-0-692-17749-5.

Printed in the United States of America.

*In gratitude to Carie Freimuth,
who was an integral part of the
Making Missionary Disciples project.*

*The Lord called her home.
May she rest in peace and may her prayers
assist us as we seek to make missionary disciples.*

CONTENTS

"By this my Father is glorified, that you bear
much fruit, and so prove to be my disciples."
(JN 15:8)

… "If any man would come after me,
let him deny himself and take up his cross
daily and follow me. …"
(LK 9:23)

"…unless a grain of wheat falls into the earth
and dies, it remains alone; but if it dies,
it bears much fruit. …"
(JN 12:24)

MAKING
MISSIONARY
DISCIPLES

INTRODUCTION

"I dream of a 'missionary option', that is, a missionary impulse capable of transforming everything…for the evangelization of today's world…"

(POPE FRANCIS, EVANGELII GAUDIUM PARA. 27)

Is this "missionary option" your dream as well? Would you like to see your parish, apostolate, or family flourishing? Do you desire to have a culture of missionary disciples who serve with great generosity and joy? Are you prepared to welcome thousands of lost and broken souls into the merciful embrace of Jesus Christ and his Church?

There is a rising awareness among Catholics that we ought to become a Church of missionary disciples. Much is being said and many wonderful programs have arisen to help make that vision a reality. But what can each of us do to experience the "needle-moving" outcomes that would result in the transformation of which Pope Francis speaks and for which we all long?

"The joy of the gospel fills the hearts and lives of all who encounter Jesus. Those who accept his offer of salvation are set free from sin, sorrow, inner emptiness and loneliness. With Christ joy is constantly born anew... I wish to encourage the Christian faithful to embark upon a new chapter of evangelization marked by this joy, while pointing out new paths for the church's journey in years to come."

(POPE FRANCIS, EVANGELII GAUDIUM PARA. 1)

Working with our bishops, and alongside amazing pastors and ministry staff on college campuses throughout the country, the missionaries and student leaders of the Fellowship of Catholic University Students (FOCUS) have much for which to be thankful. In our 20 years of work on college campuses, we have been blessed to witness amazing fruit in the lives of young people. Beginning with just 20 students on one college campus in 1998, we have seen

now more than 40,000 students who have partici-
pated in our program — and today, we are witness-
ing how the apostolate is having an impact overseas.
We recognize that the numbers themselves are not
overwhelming, since there are 70 million Catholics in the U.S. alone. There is a lot more work to be
done, though the momentum and the quality of the
individual stories points to something that offers
great hope.

While we have made many mistakes along the
way and still have much to learn, we pray that we will
continue to help reach more souls by learning both
from the example of other successful ministries and
apostolates, and from our own shortcomings, suc-
cesses, and failures. What I am about to share with
you in *Making Missionary Disciples* is simply a summa-
ry of a few key insights and approaches we have tak-
en in raising up missionary disciples that have been
a tremendous blessing in our work. We hope you
will find some helpful insights for your own work in
evangelization as well.

The Priority: Forming Missionary Disciples

Working in an environment that could be called one
of the most hostile to religion in our culture—the

university campus—FOCUS has seen the Church flourish and grow. While programs are vitally important, our work has confirmed, over and over, that *people* are everything. Everything begins to change when a *culture* of missionary disciples is established (cf. Mt 5:13-16). As the saying goes, "Culture eats strategy for breakfast." When a plan to foster missionary disciples is implemented in your parish, apostolate, or family, lives are changed, churches come alive, and poverty in all its forms begins to be addressed.

"In the end, evangelization means to set out with Christ in order to pass on the gift we have received, to transform poverty of every kind."

(JOSEPH CARDINAL RATZINGER, GOSPEL, CATECHESIS, CATECHISM: SIDELIGHTS ON THE CATECHISM OF THE CATHOLIC CHURCH P. 44)

So, if culture is the key, how do you change the culture? This idea can be a bit daunting. I am reminded of the comedian Steve Martin, who once gave a list of ten things you need to do to become a millionaire: "Step number one: Get a million dollars." Part of the problem is, how do you get started? A good start built on a clear vision will make all the difference. Let us begin with the end in mind so we can better see where it is we want to go.

Faithfulness and Fruitfulness

Over the two decades of our mission to university students, we have noticed that some of our efforts have borne more fruit, while others have borne less. "Why?" we asked ourselves. Was it a difference in execution? Was it in our missionaries? Were there other variables that would have helped us yield more fruit instead of less? We were always willing to accept less fruit, because every soul is worth the effort—but with all things being equal, we would prefer to bear more fruit rather than less.

"By this my Father is glorified, that you bear much fruit, and so prove to be my disciples."

(JN 15:8)

Evangelizing and disciple-making are much like farming: Ultimately, God controls the harvest, but there are principles and activities which good farmers utilize and which lesser farmers do not. Over time, more skilled farmers will tend to out-produce their less-skilled counterparts, even if the results vary in any given year.

Through this lens, we looked at the harvest the Lord was bringing about. Were there any patterns of success, and if so, why did those patterns exist? What were the various inputs (the things we were doing) that led to the outcomes (changed lives) for which we were praying and working so hard? How can we learn from those patterns?

After consulting with our missionaries, evaluating our inputs and outcomes, and even hiring an outside researcher to evaluate the long-term impact of our efforts, we have grown in our understanding of the key *habits* in our missionaries that helped them be more effective in evangelization and the *approaches* they took that had the biggest impact for raising up missionary disciples.

In the first half of this book, we will consider the three foundational *habits* that stand out in fostering effective evangelization. Those habits are centered on a missionary disciple's commitment to three things: Divine Intimacy, Authentic Friendship, and Clarity and Conviction about Spiritual Multiplication. We will explain each of these three habits and why they are so crucial for evangelizing, transforming lives, and building a culture of encounter and witness.

In the second half of the book, we will unpack the three-phased *approach* to evangelization our missionaries employ. We call it the "Method Modeled by the Master." The approach is not our own: It is modeled by Jesus in the Gospels and rooted in magisterial teaching on evangelization and catechesis. As we will discuss more below, the three-phased approach can be summed up in three words—"win, build, send"— which are echoed by Pope Francis in his explanation of "Encounter," "Accompaniment," and "Spirit-filled Evangelizers." When our missionaries follow this three-fold approach modeled by Jesus, they tend to be most fruitful.

"To create a culture of encounter and witness, we must live explicit lives of discipleship. We are called not only to believe in the Gospel but to allow it to take deep root in us in a way that leaves us incapable of silence: we cannot help but to announce the Gospel in word and in deed. This missionary outreach is at the heart of discipleship."

(UNITED STATES CONFERENCE OF CATHOLIC BISHOPS, LIVING AS MISSIONARY DISCIPLES: A RESOURCE FOR EVANGELIZATION P. 14)

We are keenly aware that there are major differences between university parishes, Newman Centers, Catholic chaplaincies, and your own parish, apostolate, or family. And yet, our more than 25,000 alumni have moved on from college and are now living their lives in parishes not unlike the one you attend. Even amid the great differences between the more than 150 campuses we serve—from Benedictine College to Harvard to other universities overseas—we have seen that, while adapting to local settings is always imperative, there remain some foundational habits and approaches to evangelization that apply in all situations—at universities big or small, in parishes suburban or rural, in mission fields in the United States or internationally—simply because they are rooted in human nature and the revelation of Jesus Christ.

What I am about to share with you here has been a blessing to us and I hope that it will bless you as well.

The Three Habits

The work of evangelization flows from who we are in Jesus Christ—from our baptismal vocation and ongoing encounter with the Lord. While we assume many qualities are needed in someone doing the work of evangelization (good moral character, generosity, joy, zeal, faithfulness to Church teaching, and compassion for souls, to name a few), there are three crucial habits that we have seen make or break long-term effectiveness in raising up missionary disciples. Effective missionary disciples must be committed to Divine Intimacy, to Authentic Friendship, and to having Clarity and Conviction about Spiritual Multiplication.

DIVINE INTIMACY

The first habit, the habit upon which everything else rests, is Divine Intimacy. Evangelization is first and foremost the work of God, and we will be fruitful in the mission of sharing the gospel only to the extent that we ourselves are abiding in deep union with him. As Jesus himself taught, he is the vine and we are the branches: "He who abides in me, and I in him, he it is that bears much fruit…" (Jn 15:5).

Pope St. John Paul II commented on this passage that "Communion with Jesus, which gives rise to the communion of Christians among themselves, is an indispensable condition for bearing fruit: 'Apart from me you can do nothing' (Jn 15:5)." (*Christifideles Laici* para. 32) The significance of Divine Intimacy is further emphasized in the very first sentence of the *Catechism of the Catholic Church* (CCC), which is a quote from Jesus Christ:

> "*Father, …this is eternal life, that they may know you, the only true God, and Jesus Christ whom you have sent.*" (CCC PROLOGUE)

This is the only definition of eternal life I have found in the Scriptures, and it comes directly from Christ. Jesus chooses to define eternal life in light of *relationship*. The English translation loses some of its impact: We only have a single verb for "knowing" in English—"to know"—and that one verb describes various things. In the Spanish language and other Romance languages, the translation offers more clarity. In Spanish, there are two words for "to know": *saber* (to know information), and *conocer* (to be acquainted with someone). When translated into Spanish, the meaning becomes clearer since Jesus uses the verb *conocer*. Eternal life is not knowing things *about* God, as important as that is; eternal life is being in relationship *with* the living God.

But Jesus did not speak English or a Romance language: He spoke Aramaic, the spoken form of Hebrew. The word Jesus actually used was *yada* (יָדַע), which has an even more powerful definition than *conocer*. *Yada* means to be in deep, intimate, life-long, life-giving, covenantal love. The first time *yada* is used in the Bible is in the book of Genesis:

> *"Now Adam knew [yada] Eve his wife, and she conceived and bore Cain…"* (GEN 4:1)

God is calling us to know him so intimately that we become family   that we might participate in his divine life and become adopted members of his perfect family: the Blessed Trinity.

"God, infinitely perfect and blessed in himself,
in a plan of sheer goodness freely created man
to make him share in his own blessed life."

(CCC 1)

Divine Intimacy is knowing Christ Jesus in this biblical sense (*yada*). It involves much more than believing the right things and following the Commandments. While having right doctrine and right practice are both essential, Jesus invites us to something deeper. We are made for an "intimate and vital" union with God (CCC 29). Jesus himself tells us that our salvation is found in knowing God in the biblical sense of knowing (Jn 17:3)—which means a lot more than knowing facts about God (e.g. "God exists"). It entails living in a deep, intimate, covenantal friendship with him. Fruitfulness in evangelization begins here.

God Transforming Us

Indeed, Jesus wants us to encounter him: to encounter his infinite love for us, his invitation to surrender our lives to him and trust him completely, his call to change and repent, his gentle mercy and forgiveness, and his healing power that transforms us and makes us more like him. Through regular, personal encounters with Jesus, we become changed. If you are dead in sin, the encounter with Christ breathes new life into you; if you have drifted away, encounters call you home. When you are living an active Catholic faith, moments of encounter guide, challenge, and inspire you to go deeper and live more like Christ.

The early Church Fathers gave us an image for how our lives are transformed in Christ. Imagine a cold steel bar and a hot burning fire. They have almost nothing in common. If you place the cold rod in the hot fire, though, something amazing begins to happen: The rod begins to take on the properties of the fire. It grows warm, it begins to glow — and if you were to take the rod out of the fire and touch it to some straw, it could actually start a fire itself.

Now imagine that the fire is God and we are the steel rod. When we are living in Christ through the sacraments and our lived encounters with him, we begin to take on the properties of God: The gifts and the fruits of the Spirit begin to manifest themselves in our lives. When people who manifest these godly qualities touch other people, they set their hearts on fire. The work of FOCUS has essentially been the work of sending out young people who are living from a place of encounter with Jesus and who manifest the gifts and fruits of the Holy Spirit. The seven gifts are "wisdom, understanding, counsel, fortitude, knowledge, piety, and fear of the Lord" (CCC 1831). The nine fruits are "love, joy, peace, patience, kindness, goodness, faithfulness, gentleness [and] self-control" (Gal 5:22-23).

How to Grow in Divine Intimacy:
Renewing the Encounter

How do we grow in Divine Intimacy and encounter Jesus anew each day? Consider the example of the first generation of Christian disciples whose work in evangelization and spreading the faith was unprecedented. They had spent three years with Jesus Christ and had just received the Holy Spirit at Pentecost. Acts 2:42 tells us of four essential practices to which the early disciples devoted themselves, and these same practices remain essential for those who want to live in Divine Intimacy and experience maximum fruitfulness:

1.   The Apostles' Teachings
2.   The Breaking of Bread (the sacraments)

3. Fellowship

4. Prayer

Through formation in the *Apostles' teachings* as passed down through the Church, we form our minds with the revelation of Christ, not allowing ourselves to be conformed to this world but to be transformed by the renewal of our minds (cf. Rom 12:1-2). Through the *sacraments* ("the breaking of bread"), we encounter Jesus most profoundly as we receive his grace. Through our *fellowship* with others, we grow in virtue, learning to encounter Christ in our Christian brothers and sisters, in our neighbor, and in the poor. Through our commitment to daily *prayer*, we come to know Jesus more as we grow in the interior life. These four habits are so foundational that they provide the structure of the *Catechism*.

All our work of evangelization necessarily flows from this Divine Intimacy. As Jesus warned, "apart from me you can do nothing" (Jn 15:5). First, we must encounter Jesus personally. Flowing from these moments of personal encounter with Jesus, these four key practices of Acts 2:42 continually pull us deeper into the fire of God's love. Living in Divine Intimacy, the missionary disciple depends on God's initiative for guidance and strength, not their own. Evangelization is ultimately the work of God, who loves us and takes the initiative to draw souls back to him. We are merely participating in that love. In the words of Pope Benedict XVI:

> "…it is important always to know that the first word, the true initiative, the true activity comes from God and only by inserting ourselves into the divine initiative, only by begging for this divine initiative, shall we too be able to become — with him and in him — evangelizers." (MEDITATION OF HIS HOLINESS POPE BENEDICT XVI DURING THE FIRST GENERAL CONGREGATION, 8 OCT. 2012)

Indeed, as Pope Paul VI emphasized, "Only your personal and profound union with Christ will assure the fruitfulness of your apostolate whatever it may be." (*Third World Congress for the Apostolate of the Laity*, 15 Oct. 1967). We can yet draw more on the Church's treasures in deepening our Divine Intimacy—and in FOCUS, we have found that there are particular practices that have helped us go deeper: daily mental prayer, frequent participation in the sacraments, Eucharistic adoration, devotion to the Blessed Virgin (particularly through the Rosary), the Divine Mercy Chaplet, spiritual reading, intellectual formation, fellowship with other disciples, service to the poor, and a willingness to step beyond our comfort zone so that God can prove his faithfulness over and over.

AUTHENTIC FRIENDSHIP

Authentic Friendship is the second habit we have come to see as essential if we want to bear fruit.

In forming missionary disciples, it is not enough to pass on the gospel message and the teachings of the Church. That is essential, but we must do more. We must genuinely love the people we are serving, accompanying them in life and personally investing ourselves in them with Authentic Friendship. This is what St. Paul modeled when he formed disciples:

> *"So, being affectionately desirous of you, we were ready to share with you not only the gospel of God but also our own selves, because you had become very dear to us."* (1 THES 2:8)

We often hear from students that one of the key contributing factors in their conversion was the sense that their Bible study leader got to know them, spent time with them outside of Bible study, listened to them, and walked beside them in life. "He/she was truly my friend," they often say. Indeed, when we genuinely love the people we serve, we offer them something not easily found in our modern world: Authentic Friendship. As Pope Francis explained, this is central to the work of evangelization in parishes, dioceses, and all other communities of faith:

> *"An evangelizing community gets involved by word and deed in people's daily lives; it bridges distances, it is willing to abase itself if necessary, and it embraces human life, touching the suffering flesh of Christ in others. Evangelizers thus take on the 'smell of the sheep' and the sheep are willing to hear their voice."*
>
> (EVANGELII GAUDIUM PARA. 24)

Pope Francis is simply echoing the way of evangelization that God himself modeled for us. God did not remain in heaven watching us from a distance. He did not just send commandments, leaders, teachers, and prophets from afar. He *did* do this, and he did still more. He personally entered our world and became one of us, taking on human flesh in Jesus Christ. Before there was a clearly defined set of Catholic doctrine, Jesus simply shared life, first with Joseph and Mary and later with his Apostles.

And all throughout his public ministry, Jesus continued to go out to meet the people in their particular circumstances. He did not passively wait in the synagogue for people to come to him. He did not make announcements about the next faith formation night he was offering. He went out to the people: to the villages—to the tax collectors' office—to the poor and sick—to the drunkards, prostitutes, and sinners. He got involved in others' lives, shared meals, sincerely took an interest in them, and took on the smell of his sheep.

In FOCUS, we call this model for sharing the faith "Incarnational Evangelization." Just as the Son of God entered our world in the incarnation to seek us out, so too must we enter into the world of the people we are serving, not passively waiting for them to come to us. We must give of ourselves in Authentic Friendship, sincerely loving them for their own sake, whether they respond to the gospel or not. Like St. Paul, we must not only share the gospel, but our very selves.

The Power of Personal Investment

One practical point flows from this theme of Authentic Friendship.

The personal time invested outside of formal faith formation sessions is often where lives are changed the most—and it is what makes formal faith formation sessions themselves more fruitful. Too often, however, we reduce the leaders in our faith communities to functions: sponsors, godparents, RCIA teachers, catechists, Bible study leaders, small-group facilitators. If you come to a few meetings and show up at someone's confirmation, you have fulfilled the minimal requirement for your function as a sponsor. If you lead your Bible study at your parish each week, you have completed your minimum functional duty as a volunteer small-group facilitator. But how much time do we spend with the people we are serving outside those formal meetings and sessions? How much do we invest in them personally, accompanying them in life, praying for their personal needs and intentions—in other words, taking on the smell of the sheep? Forming disciples and investing in them personally was not just a job for Jesus. It was a whole way of life. It should be for us as well. While the functions just listed may be essential, reducing discipleship to functionality will limit (or even possibly eliminate) our fruitfulness.

When Pope St. John Paul II was a young priest in Poland, he did not just teach people from the pulpit or in a classroom. He spent a lot of time with a few people, accompanying them in daily life: sharing meals, singing, performing plays, hiking, camping, kayaking. Those shared moments outside of formal faith formation sessions contributed to a more profound, lasting impact on those young people than his homilies, classroom lectures, and books ever could have had on their own. And he remained close friends with these people all the way to the end of his life. Similarly, taking time outside of Bible study, RCIA, or sacramental preparation classes to truly get to know the people we serve, to take an interest in their lives, to listen to them and share life with them will do much more for evangelization than any adult faith formation class can do in isolation. Going for coffee, sharing meals, working out together, volunteering together, serving the poor together, praying together, hanging out, or simply listening: These are just a few examples of how to practice the art of accompaniment.

CLARITY AND CONVICTION ABOUT SPIRITUAL MULTIPLICATION

This third habit is impossible without the first two. Divine Intimacy breathes Christ's life into us so that it is God's work and not our own. Authentic Friendship is the setting in which we do the work of evangelization—not functionally as a program, but relationally, in the context of accompaniment. While we can (and should) do many good things in life, we should never let those things distract or keep us from deep, Christ-centered friendships with a relative few, lived in such a way that we impart not only faithfulness, but also fruitfulness. It is through this simple approach that we can reach the world in every generation—and Clarity and Conviction about Spiritual Multiplication is that laser focus which keeps us on task: *clarity* that this is the most effective way to fulfill the Great Commission to make disciples of all nations (Mt 28:19), and *conviction* that we must prioritize our actions to make time for these relationships.

So, what is Spiritual Multiplication? Spiritual Multiplication is exemplified by Jesus, who invested deeply in a remarkably few disciples and trained them to do the same so that the whole world could be reached with the Gospel. In the Great Commission, Jesus said to his disciples, "All authority in heaven and on earth has been given to me. Go therefore and make disciples *of all nations* ..." (Mt 28:18-19, emph. added). How could this small group of disciples possibly reach all the nations? It was not by developing a spectacular faith formation program that could be translated in all languages, or organizing a global conference with gifted speakers, or designing a catchy video that could go viral on the internet. These can be wonderful tools at the service of evangelization, but the heart of what the disciples were commissioned to do is what Jesus had done: to make disciples—to invest in a few people so as to form them as followers of Jesus and equip them to go out and do the same for others.

The 2 Timothy 2:2 Principle

Consider again the great missionary apostle St. Paul. He traveled the known world speaking to large crowds and inviting multitudes to faith in Christ. But, like Jesus, he traveled with a small group of men with whom he deeply shared his life. He formed them as his disciples. One of these men was St. Timothy. After having spent years together, they were separated and Paul was sent to prison, awaiting his martyrdom. He wrote to Timothy and reminded him of the importance of imparting not just faithfulness, but also fruitfulness:

> "...what you have heard from me before many witnesses entrust to faithful men who will be able to teach others also." (2 TIM 2:2)

In FOCUS, we call this the 2 Timothy 2:2 principle. This verse challenges us to keep our focus on forming not just disciples, but *missionary* disciples. Paul saw that his mission was not simply to get Timothy to go to Mass on Sunday, live a good moral life, and grow in holiness, as important as those are. Paul was raising up Timothy as a missionary disciple— someone who would go out and form disciples of his own and equip them to do the same for others. In other words, Paul formed Timothy not just to be faithful, but also *fruitful* and to impart faithfulness and fruitfulness to others. And here is the key: forming *missionary* disciples was so important for St. Paul that in his last letter from prison to Timothy, he urgently reminds his own disciple to teach his disciples to teach others.

There are three generations of discipleship here in 2 Timothy 2:2:

First Generation:
Paul → Timothy

Second Generation:
Timothy → Timothy's Disciples

Third Generation:
Timothy's Disciples → Their Disciples

Feel the weight of this. St. Paul cares about not just the first generation of faith formation—Timothy— but he is also thinking about the *next* generation and how Timothy will form his disciples to follow Jesus.

But it does not stop there. Paul is so concerned about passing on the vision of missionary discipleship that he specifically reminds Timothy to make sure his own disciples pass on the faith to others. Paul is thinking about the third generation. When a missionary disciple imparts faith-filled fruitfulness, they foster an ever-growing chain of missionary disciples.

Much faith formation today focuses just on the first generation—namely, the people showing up in our pews and to our programs. If faith formation is going well, we are forming people as disciples. But what are we doing to form them as *missionary* disciples? We certainly must lead people to fall in love with Jesus. Spiritual Multiplication helps them fall in love with his mission.

In the next section, we will delve deeper into the approach itself—the three-phased Method Modeled by the Master—and explore how to live in such a way as to impart both faithfulness and fruitfulness. For now, I would like to share how this way of living offers the greatest opportunity for fruitfulness compared to any other method or program we have seen for raising up missionary disciples. Having clarity and conviction about living this way has yielded much fruit.

It is essential to note that this method is fundamentally relational, and any attempt to demonstrate the eventual effectiveness will run the risk of sounding formulaic. To reduce this method to a formula would be a devastating mistake. We have seen that, when we solely examine the process and lose sight of Divine Intimacy and Authentic Friendship, fruitfulness is lost. At the same time, when we live the first two habits without the third, we also hinder our ability to bear as much fruit as we could.

You Can Change the World

Spiritual Multiplication is shockingly simple, yet extraordinarily powerful. A person with clarity and conviction for it may have many friends and acquaintances, but their deep-seated desire to live as a missionary disciple leads them to form just a handful of very deep friendships. As a missionary disciple, they play the role of an older brother or sister to a few others—not competing with the spiritual fatherhood of the pastor or other parish leaders, but rather complementing their roles. (I have seen this work in my own family as my older children have loved and helped their younger siblings.) As the missionary disciple begins to work with a few friends who are living from a place of encounter, they all agree to do whatever it takes to become saints and help each other become saints. As they share life together, they begin to mature in their faithfulness. After some time, the original missionary disciple invites the friends they have been mentoring to go beyond faithfulness and to live fruitfulness by going out and repeating the process. Each of those friends then finds a small number of people in whom *they* can invest.

We have been inviting university students to follow this habit of faithfulness and fruitfulness for more than 20 years. With this simple model in mind, I would like to paint a picture of what the impact can look like in real life. (For the sake of demonstration, I will use the number three; in our experience, the number of people with whom someone works will vary, usually ranging from three to eight — but the impact from just three is incredible.)

Let us consider an imaginary parish in an imaginary city and see how Spiritual Multiplication can change the culture and world. Our imaginary parish has 4,000 Catholics and 19,000 people in total within its geographical boundary, and the parish is located in a city of 500,000.[1] Now we can illustrate the impact that just one person could have on the parish, the city, and the world.

---

1   There are approximately 323,000,000 people in the U.S. and approximately 17,000 parishes. So, on average, there are approximately 19,000 people living within the boundaries of each parish and the national average shows that 22% of Americans self-identify as Catholic.

Like I described previously, a single missionary disciple begins working with three "younger" disciples who are committed to following Christ and the Church and dedicated to living in Divine Intimacy and Authentic Friendship. The goal at this stage is to deepen their encounter with Christ and, over time, form them in their faith and life so that they too would go out and lead others to Christ. Eventually, these three first-generation disciples will go out and work with a small number of disciples of their own. (We have seen this cycle typically take six to eighteen months on college campuses, but it can be shorter or longer, depending on each individual and their response to the Holy Spirit's timing.) Once each of the three have gone out and each found three more, the total number of missionary disciples increases by nine, adding up to 13 missionary disciples—that is the original missionary disciple, plus the three in whom they invested (for a total of four people), plus the nine new second-generation disciples. After another cycle of formation, the nine new missionary disciples are encouraged to go out and repeat the process starting a third generation of missionary disciples, reaching 27 new missionary disciples for a total of 40.

Just like Paul with Timothy, the number of people reached multiplies through the generations.

First Generation: 1 → 3
Second Generation: 3 → 9
Third Generation: 9 → 27

So far, the visible impact is not too noticeable; the 40 missionary disciples in a parish of 4,000 is not enough to transform the culture of the parish. However, the lives of these 40 people, along with their families, are beginning to experience dramatic change, and a culture of missionary discipleship is now ready to emerge.[2]

Imagine what happens if each subsequent generation of missionary disciples begins bearing fruit like the others before them. The impact of Spiritual Multiplication can be astounding. In the seventh generation, 243 missionary disciples will begin sharing life with 729 new disciples, and the total number of parishioners will reach 1,093—i.e., one in four members of the parish. The ever-expanding fruitfulness is not only changing lives, but is also starting to change the wider culture.

Note that, because growth is incremental—one

---

2   Note that during this time, the first missionary disciple is still investing in the three first-generation disciples, and those three are investing in the nine second-generation disciples. The key is to continue to care for caregivers, to feed those who are feeding others.

person reaching out to three—even in a large parish, every individual person involved in discipleship is known, loved, and cared for. The large parish is a unified body, filled with healthy cells of deep, authentic friendships, all growing closer to Jesus. By the ninth cycle, there will be more missionary disciples than there are Catholics within the parish boundaries, and their overflow will begin reaching out to non-Catholics, if that has not already occurred. These converts will come and experience a Church unlike any they have imagined, filled with vibrant believers who invest deeply into the lives of others. By the thirteenth cycle, the entire city of 500,000 would be reached, and in 22 cycles, the world. This beautifully illustrates the amazing potential impact one person can have in changing the world!

But let me be clear. The actual numbers should not distract us. Focusing on the numbers can divert our attention from the beauty, simplicity, and heart of the model. The crucial thing for us is that we love God and the few people he places in our lives—and that we impart faithfulness *and* fruitfulness. The numbers simply serve to illustrate what can happen if we follow the Method Modeled by the Master. Spiritual Multiplication is the method of evangelization modeled by Jesus and which can reach this generation of people in this lifetime, providing the opportunity for everyone to come to faith in Christ, embrace membership in the Church, and be known, loved, and cared for in a personal way. Those with Clarity and Conviction about Spiritual Multiplication must be committed to the other two foundational habits— Divine Intimacy and Authentic Friendship—if they want to be fruitful. There will, of course, be failures along the way, but these failures will likely be the result of a breakdown in one of these three habits.

* * *

God deeply desires for every person in each generation to come to know his love and mercy. He modeled the method to make this possible, and then he commissioned us to imitate him by making disciples. We can now take a closer look at this three-phased approach to raising up missionary disciples. By following Christ's method of evangelization, along with cultivating the three foundational habits just discussed, we will be able to respond to the urgency of the call. This generation is waiting for us to become what we were meant to be. Everyone on earth is experiencing poverty of some kind, and they are waiting to be cared for by people who have experienced the enriching reality of life in Christ.

The Method Modeled

by the Master

Raising Up Missionary Disciples
Who Change the World

"The harvest is plentiful, but the laborers are few;
pray therefore to the Lord of the harvest…"

(Lk 10:2)

"I sense that the moment has come to commit all of
the Church's energies to a new evangelization and to
the mission ad gentes. No believer in Christ, no in-
stitution of the Church can avoid this supreme duty:
to proclaim Christ to all peoples."

(Pope St. John Paul II, Redemptoris Missio sec. 3)

We live in a moment of great opportunity. There has never been a time when there have been more vibrant, engaging, and faithful catechetical resources available in such abundance. The Augustine Institute, Dynamic Catholic, The St. Paul Center for Biblical Theology, Eternal Word Television Network (EWTN), Word on Fire, Ascension Press, Ignatius Press, and many other organizations have helped change the landscape of catechesis. Other programs such as Cursillo, Christ Renews His Parish (CRHP), The Amazing Parish, and Alpha are available to ignite renewal within parishes — and many others provide parish leaders with a wide variety of options for engaging the faithful and evangelizing new members. This is good news for a Church seeking renewal, as the Catechism teaches:

> *"Periods of renewal in the Church are also intense moments of catechesis."* (CCC 8)

At the same time, many parishes have experienced frustration in their efforts to utilize these tools effectively. You may ask, "What is wrong with the tools?" I would respond, "Nothing. The tools are great — we just have a problem with our culture." Our strategies, efforts, and programs do not bear the fruit we desire because, while we have a renewed desire for evangelization and disciple-making, our parish cultures have yet to become evangelizing, disciple-making cultures. As pastoral leaders know, the best of catechetical resources can never replace the living witness of a missionary disciple leading others into a deeper union with Christ and the Church. Many parishes, unfortunately, are not capable of fully benefiting from these programs because there is not a critical mass of missionary disciples to utilize the tools effectively, give witness to the gospel, and accompany people through the process of conversion.

So, what can be done to light the fire of our culture so that our parishes, apostolates, and families become receptive? We would like to think that this work is already underway through the work the Holy Spirit is doing in raising up many young people to serve as the future leaders of the Church. We have witnessed first-hand the amazing work so many priests, religious, chaplains, and lay campus ministers throughout the country are doing on college campuses, inspiring and forming the next generation of Catholic leaders.

Many bishops have recognized that the majority of young leaders for our parishes, apostolates, and families will pass through our universities. They will become seminarians and later priests; religious women and men; mothers and fathers of the next generation; Catholic school teachers; parish volunteers; staff members and financial donors: In a word, they will become *disciples* whose lives revolve around their faith in Christ and their love for one another. If young leaders are not evangelized and cared for, they will be less engaged at every level, which will weaken our Church and society for years to come. Aware of this, those bishops have made the strategic decision to place some of their most joy-filled, evangelistically minded (and frequently young) priests in the role of campus ministry. And while much more is needed than simply a faithful priest who loves his priesthood and his people, there is no replacement for him. As someone who has been involved in the lay apostolate for 25 years, I can say with conviction that the priest is the single greatest factor in fruitfulness and effectiveness here.

There are other fine organizations doing great work on university campuses such as Saint Paul's Outreach, Evangelical Catholic, and Catholic Christian Outreach, and they have thousands of alumni as well. There are also alumni from great youth apostolates like Life Teen and Steubenville Youth Conferences, in addition to the many faithful members of groups like the Knights of Columbus and ENDOW. We have seen the fruit in FOCUS as well: More than 25,000 of our alumni are now living and working in parishes, serving other apostolates, bringing the gospel to their spheres of influence in the Church and in the world, and raising families. More than 700 of these alumni have made the decision to discern a vocation to the priesthood or religious life.

There are plenty of sparks from which to start the fire. Imagine the impact these living witnesses could have on parish life: thousands of men and women who are on fire for the faith and equipped to lead others to an encounter with Christ—indeed, thousands of missionary disciples who are available to assist clergy and lay parish leaders in their mission of evangelization. We must ask the question, "Is there a way to activate their desire to be even more fruitful?" Those who have experienced the first fruits of the new evangelization are poised to catalyze pivotal change in the Church and broader culture.

An Army of Missionary Disciples

Every parish church is unique, as are the neighborhoods they serve. With this great diversity, how can there be a single solution that fits and serves all parishes, apostolates, and families? I would propose an analogy. The amazing diversity we find in people is awe-inspiring: billions of people over millennia, and no two of them are the same, not even "identical" twins. The countless factors which influence diversity stagger the mind: gender, ethnicity, cultural norms, personality — the list goes on and on. Yet, despite this diversity, we have bone structures that are remarkably similar. Our skeletons provide support and a framework for our bodies to function. So, akin to a human skeleton, might there also be some fundamental principles that could provide reliable support and a framework for the renewal of our parishes, which would also allow us some consistency amidst all the amazing diversity?

"… the vital core of the new evangelization must be a clear and unequivocal proclamation of the person of Jesus Christ, that is, the preaching of his name, his teaching, his life, his promises and the Kingdom which he has gained for us by his Paschal Mystery."

(POPE ST. JOHN PAUL II, ECCLESIA IN AMERICA SEC. 66)

One constant, fundamental principle that applies in all settings of the Church's mission is Jesus' model for evangelization. At the heart of Jesus' public ministry, there were a handful of people with whom Jesus lived. He shared his life with them, he spoke with them, he walked with them over many, many miles—and even when he was with the multitudes, these 12 Apostles were right at his side. Jesus lived a life of authentic friendship with a relative few, and he imparted both faithfulness and fruitfulness. This simple mode of living can be imitated by almost anyone—and, as we will see, it unleashes the capacity to transform lives, renew parishes, and reach the world.

But Jesus not only modeled this method; he commissioned us to follow his example. With his final words on earth—after his death, after his resurrection, on the last of the 40 days and moments before his ascension into heaven—Jesus said:

> *"All authority in heaven and on earth has been given to me. Go therefore and make disciples of all nations, baptizing them in the name of the Father and of the Son and of the Holy Spirit, teaching them to observe all that I have commanded you; and lo, I am with you always, to the close of the age."* (MT 28:18-20)

This would appear to be the most authoritative statement ever made. Yes, Jesus is God, and everything he says is completely authoritative—but among his sayings, it seems that he highlights some statements over others. Sometimes Jesus will highlight importance with his phrasing. For example, when speaking about baptism in John Chapter 3 or the Eucharist in John Chapter 6, Jesus utilizes oath language, saying, "Truly, truly"—or, depending on the translation, "Verily, verily" or "Amen, amen" (Jn 3:3, 6:32). In other places, Jesus highlights the significance of his words by the setting within which he says them. For example, his words at the Last Supper would appear to be all the more meaningful given the context. In the case of the Great Commission, Jesus does both. The context is his farewell address, and his wording is provocative. He begins by saying "All authority in heaven and earth has been given to me." Jesus is the only one in the history of the world who could have said this, and he only says it once, so what follows must be important.

One of the simple interpretive tools we share with the FOCUS missionaries is this: When you see the word "therefore" in the Bible, stop and look back to see what it is "there for." The word is a connector, and it unites two themes. In this case, the two themes are these: "All authority" and "make disciples." Jesus has just given us an authoritative commission. Yet, we might be tempted to take it as a mere suggestion. We might be tempted to think that organizing events, creating programs, and holding meetings could be an acceptable alternative to making disciples. Those endeavors certainly can be at the service of discipleship—but the heart of the Great Commission is forming disciples. It is the way of life that Jesus modeled for us, and he commissions us to follow that model and evangelize like he did.

So, let us take a closer look at the Method Modeled by the Master, an approach that has three key phases that can be summed up as "win, build, send" or, in the language of Pope Francis, as "Encounter", "Accompaniment," and "Spirit-filled Evangelizers" (cf. Pope Paul VI, *Ecclesiam Suam*).

Win: Leading Souls to Encounter Christ

In this first step of forming missionary disciples, we lead people to a life-shaping encounter with Jesus Christ. Jesus went to the tax collector's office and called Matthew to follow him. Philip, after encountering Jesus himself, went and told Nathaniel, who then experienced his own transformative encounter with Christ. Jesus met the Samaritan woman at the well, revealed to her that he was the Messiah and inspired her to repentance. We are called to lead people to a similar encounter with the living Jesus today, one that entails much more than merely going through the motions with our faith (going to Mass, believing the right doctrines, saying some prayers, and avoiding serious sin). All that is essential, but God wants more for us than merely following the rules. God wants us to live in relationship with him and every other aspect of our faith exists to serve our relationship with the living God. That is the key question: Am I living in friendship with Jesus Christ? Is he truly the center of my life, or are other things more important? As we tell college students, if Jesus is not Lord of all, he is not Lord at all.

A friend of mine once told me that, in his experience, many Catholics live in a "loveless marriage with God." Because of baptism and their minimal practicing of the faith, they are in covenant with God—but the love, joy, and goodness of the friendship is not there. They might go through the motions with their faith, but are they growing in a deeper love? Evangelization is all about inviting people into friendship with Jesus Christ, inviting them to entrust their lives to him, welcoming Jesus as the very center and Lord of their lives.

The key to the "win" is facilitating moments of encounter with Christ, for living in right relationship with God is the heart of Christianity. Encounters are those experiences where people leave lasting impressions in our lives. I remember the first time I met my wife; I remember our first kiss; I have had many encounters with her over the years, and they shape the love story that is our marriage. In some cases, an encounter can move us from having no relationship into having a new and amazing relationship. In other cases, encounters strengthen existing relationships.

A few months ago, my father passed away. I was there with my mother and my only brother. My dad died at about 2:00 in the morning. After he passed, we sat up for hours, laughing and crying, remembering different times we had been with him and our memories of him. Those encounters were the foundations of our relationship with him. In the same way, our encounters with God form the foundations of our relationship with him.

In fact, the Gospels themselves can be seen as a series of encounters which are being recounted for our sake. As we read the Gospels, we are reading the memories of the Apostles under the inspiration of the Holy Spirit. You can almost imagine the Apostles thinking, "Remember that time Jesus gave that sermon on the mountain, or the time he forgave that woman who had been caught in adultery?" The various encounters they had with Jesus formed their friendship with him and transformed their lives. Our ability to encounter the risen Jesus today—through the teachings of the apostles, fellowship, the sacraments, and prayer (cf. Acts 2:42)—is what allows us to deepen our friendship with him and transforms our lives as well.

Sharing the Gospel: Winning Hearts for Christ

But how do we facilitate encounters with Christ that lead to conversion? How do we "win" people to friendship with Christ? First, as the Church emphasizes, it is through our witness. Pope Paul VI said:

> "Modern man listens more willingly to witnesses than to teachers, and if he does listen to teachers, it is because they are witnesses." (Evangelii Nuntiandi para. 41)

The witness of an authentic Christian life attracts others. Especially in a lonely, self-centered secular world, the joy of the Christian life stands out. We hear this repeatedly from the young people who convert on college campuses. They tell us that the joy and love our missionaries exhibited is what initially drew them to consider the Catholic faith: "They have something I want, but don't have."

Second, we must share with people not only the gospel but our very selves (cf. 1 Thes 2:8). As we saw when discussing Authentic Friendship, we must invest ourselves personally in the people we serve, entering their world, accompanying them outside of formal faith formation settings, and taking on the smell of the sheep. We must win the right to be heard and always love the people we serve unconditionally, regardless of whether they become committed Catholics.

Third, as much as witness, example, hospitality, and personal investment are crucial means of evangelization, the Church teaches it is not enough. As Pope Paul VI said:

> "Nevertheless, [witness] always remains insufficient because even the finest witness will prove ineffective in the long run if it is not explained, justified ... and made explicit by a clear and unequivocal proclamation of the Lord Jesus." (EVANGELII NUNTIANDI PARA. 22)

If we want to be faithful to the Church's mission of evangelization, we must again recall what Pope Paul VI taught us: "Preaching, the verbal proclamation of the message is indeed always indispensable." (Evangelii Nuntiandi para. 42). We must share the gospel message and invite people to surrender their lives to Christ, putting Jesus first.

Sharing the Gospel: The Message

To be effective in sharing the good news, we need to communicate the heart of the gospel: simply put, the

fact that God loves us and has a plan for our lives—
that even though we turned away from him, he still
loved us so much that he became one of us in Jesus
Christ, died for us, and rose again so that we might
have new life in him in his Church. He wants to be-
stow his mercy upon us and offer us a much better
life than what we experience without him. He offers
eternal life, happiness forever with him in heaven.

One way of summing up the proclamation of the
gospel is this: sharing the *good* news, the *bad* news,
and the *even better* news and to invite people to join
the adventure.

The good news: You were created to be amazing! As
St. Catherine of Siena put it, "If you are what you were
meant to be, you would set the world on fire." You
were actually conceived twice—first in the mind of
God, as Scripture tells us:

> *"…he [the Father] chose us in him [the Son] before the*
> *foundation of the world…"* (EPH. 1:4)

God loved the idea of you so much that, at the
chosen time, you were conceived a second time, just
under your mother's heart when your life began.

The bad news: You are not who you were meant to
be. Sin has wounded you and separated you from
God. Our problem is actually far worse than we

might have imagined. At first glance, we may think that, with some effort toward self-improvement, we could close the gap between who we are and who we ought to be. It is simply not the case. When we fell:

The fall was *universal*—

"All have sinned and fall short of the glory of God." *(Rom 3:23)*

The fall was *severe*—

"For the wages of sin is death." (Rom 6:23)

The fall created a chasm so great that no human could bridge it even with the best of efforts.

Through St. Catherine of Siena, we are reminded that:

"... the road was broken by the sin and disobedience of Adam, in such a way, that no one could arrive at Eternal Life." (The Dialogue of St. Catherine of Siena)

| Humanity | God |

The even better news: While we were unable to save ourselves, "God so loved the world that he gave his only Son, that whoever believes in him should not perish but have eternal life." (Jn 3:16). Turning to St. Catherine of Siena, Pope Benedict XVI explained that "… she describes Christ, with an unusual image, as a bridge flung between Heaven and earth." (*General Audience*, 24 November 2010). The life, death and resurrection of Jesus is God's only remedy for our sin (cf. Acts 4:12).

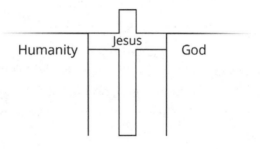

Jesus lived, died, and rose from the dead for you so that you can become who you were meant to be. When we see what Jesus went through for each of us, two fundamental truths come to light. One: If that is what it took to save us, we must have been in pretty bad shape. And two: If that is what it took to save us, Jesus must think we are worth the effort.

Salvation is a gift, freely offered to each of us by

God. Before a gift can be owned, though, it must be accepted. The decision to accept God's saving gift means making the fundamental choice to become a disciple of Jesus. God's gift is a complete gift of himself to you and for you; the only appropriate response is a complete gift of ourselves in return.

When we accept God's gift of salvation, we begin to listen to what he says and do what he asks. As we do so, we experience renewal. Our culture will be renewed when there are sufficient number of people in the culture who have been renewed. Following Jesus means to begin seeking to "love the Lord your God with all your heart, and with all your soul, and with all your might" (Deut 6:5).

Build: Accompanying Disciples

Once someone has surrendered their life to the Lordship of Jesus, it is critical to build them up in their faith, and friendship is the context in which that takes place most effectively. Saints come in clusters. Think of St. Paul, St. Timothy, and St. Titus—or St. Monica, St. Ambrose, and St. Augustine—or St. Francis and St. Clare–or St. Ignatius, St. Francis Xavier, and St. Peter Faber. The influence of friendship is hard to overstate. Just as bad company corrupts good morals, godly company facilitates godliness. Sound teaching is imperative, but it is not sufficient.

In the Method Modeled by the Master, Jesus shares his life with his disciples. Even before his public ministry, the investment he made in the Blessed Virgin Mary (and St. Joseph) is breathtaking. Remember, even though he had the greatest mission in human history, he was 30 years old and living at home—but far from keeping Jesus from his mission, his home life was the nearest thing to the Garden of Eden since the Fall. Jesus was God, Mary was sinless, and Joseph was a just man: Life was lived beautifully in their home in Nazareth.

In both his hidden life and public ministry, Jesus models an awe-inspiring commitment to personal relationships. When we are asked, "How much time does discipleship take?" we respond, "All of it." Or, as St. Paul wrote to the Church he founded in Thessalonica, reminding them how he formed them as missionary disciples:

"So, being affectionately desirous of you, we were ready to share with you not only the gospel of God but also our own selves, because you had become very dear to us." (1 THES 2:8)

Those things in life that are the most natural are

learned by modeling, not by mere instruction. Taking our first steps and speaking our first words, for example, were learned simply by living with people who walked and spoke. Holiness is meant to be learned the same way. Yes, there is a need for instruction—but demonstration is much more effective than explanation. We need to spend time with people who are living from a place of encounter and walk with them. As we seek to live as missionary disciples, we learn from one another, we motivate one another, we forgive one another, and we love one another.

It is within these close relationships that mentoring occurs. Mentorship facilitates the maturing of new followers of Jesus who have begun to live from a place of encounter into disciplined followers of Christ. For friendship to become discipleship, there must be an explicit choice to place Christ at the center of the human relationships and to make the common pursuit of holiness the primary aim of the friendship.

Relationship is everything. Our relationship with God and with others is both our salvation and our destiny. It is in the midst of relationship with others that we can ask and answer two fundamental questions: What do I need to learn so that I can think with the mind of Christ, and how do I need to be formed to live with the character of Christ? The deep investment required for this type of formation means it must be undertaken with just a few people. It might be possible to be loving toward a large group, but to truly love individuals deeply, the number must be limited. Jesus was God, and he chose only 12 men—and even then, he spent some key moments with just Peter, James, and John. Even when he spoke to the multitudes, his trusted friends were right there with him. Within a life of accompaniment, we learn to live lives open to the workings of the Holy Spirit, and as we entrust ourselves to the Holy Spirit, we can be sent out to become Spirit-filled evangelists and multipliers.

How to Build

There are three things we do at this "build" stage that we find helpful for preparing someone for the work of evangelization.

First, we help the person live more deeply, day to day, as a true disciple of Christ. What the person has initially begun to embrace at the "win" stage should now become a habit in "build." Indeed, the four practices of the earliest disciples in Acts 2:42 should become their own. We feed their minds through discipleship, reading, retreats, and other faith formation opportunities so that they will not be conformed to this world but be transformed by Christ and *the teaching of the Apostles*. We urge them to frequent the *sacraments*, participating in daily Mass when they can, in regular confession (once a month), in visits to the Blessed Sacrament, and in Eucharistic adoration. We encourage them to grow in virtue and friendship so that they might be strengthened in Christian *fellowship*. And as they are taking time for *prayer* (20-30 minutes a day), we help deepen their practice and understanding of prayer and their cultivating an interior life. This continuous deepening in Divine Intimacy is the key foundation upon which their mission of evangelization depends.

Second, we must train disciples on how to evangelize and model it for them ourselves. There are many skills and approaches that make for effective evangelization: how to share the gospel message, how to share your testimony, how to lead an effective small group, how to mentor others in the discipleship relationship, etc. Here, we begin to pull back the veil, so to speak, and talk about many of the things we or others did for them in their own conversion and deepening in faith.

But it is not enough just to *talk* about these things. We must also *show* them how to do it through our example. *Teaching is essential, but it is not sufficient.* As St. Paul said, "Be imitators of me as I am of Christ"

(1 Cor 11:1). There is an expression we like to use in FOCUS that expresses this point well: "More is caught than taught." When people observe the way we evangelize, some of that begins to rub off on them. The ideas they have heard you teach them begin to take deeper root as they see in you a concrete example of how to do it. Much more powerful than a workshop on evangelization is inviting someone to join you as you share the joy of Christ with others.

What are some ways to do this? Invite a disciple to come with you when you go to the chapel to pray for the people you are serving. Ask the disciple to come with you when you go do outreach in your neighborhood, visit the sick, or hang out with some of the people in your Bible study. Have your disciple attend a small group you lead or a faith formation class you teach. These are just some of many ways we walk with our disciples and model the life of missionary discipleship. Remember, "more is caught than taught."

Third, give the disciple incremental opportunities to practice leadership. When you invite them to accompany you on mission, perhaps you can give them a role to play. After watching how you lead a small group session one week, they might be able to lead a part of that small group the following week.

The next time you teach a class, perhaps you can have them give a short three-minute reflection for the group at the end of the session. Think of ways to give your disciple small experiences in evangelization and leadership before they launch out on their own. This can help boost their confidence. It also gives you the chance to offer some constructive feedback on what they did well and how they can improve. All this helps prepare them to go out confidently and effectively as missionary disciples who are leading others to Christ.

Send: Launching Spirit-Filled Evangelists and Multipliers

After the Great Commission, the disciples were huddled in the Upper Room with Mary until Jesus sent the Holy Spirit to them on Pentecost. With the Holy Spirit, they were able to go out boldly, apply their training, and share the good news with the world. They moved from being just disciples to disciple makers. This final phase of the Method Modeled by the Master is not possible without the Encounter or Accompaniment, without Win or Build. However, this is the phase which opens up the good news to the world so that we can address poverty in all of its forms and invite everyone to know and experience the love and mercy of God through the Church.

In our experience, this is where the culture within Christian communities begins to change. As disciples become disciple makers, they come alive in their faith in entirely new ways. As people begin to invest in others, those who do the investing come even more alive. While we are grateful that most of the students we serve remain active in their faith after graduation, there is a measurable, long-term increase in their faithfulness (participation in Church activities), alignment (agreement with Church teaching on countercultural topics), and engagement (continued investment in helping others encounter Jesus and then accompanying them) if they became disciple makers while in college.

What is clear is that gathering disciples for faith formation is not enough. Are we *sending* disciples on mission? As we have seen, Jesus did not just form his disciples: He commissioned them to go out and "make disciples for all nations" (Mt 28:19). Similarly, St. Paul did not just pass on good Christian teaching and practices to his disciples: He sent them to go out and find other trustworthy people to train them to do the same for others (2 Tim 2:2)—in other words, he trained his disciples to become disciple makers.

How long does it take to move from being a new-
ly evangelized or re-evangelized Christian living in
a place of Encounter into living in Accompaniment
and then becoming a Spirit-filled Evangelizer? It var-
ies. We have seen it take years, and we have seen it
take only a few weeks. What is necessary to under-
stand is that becoming a disciple maker does not just
happen, it comes about from a "second conversion"
just as the encounter comes about by a conversion
of heart and accepting the saving gift of Jesus' death
and resurrection; embracing a willingness to do
anything and suffer any consequence to follow Jesus
and embrace his salvation. The decision to become
a disciple maker is a deepening of unity with Christ,
not only to be willing to do anything to embrace
Christ but the willingness to do anything so that
others may embrace Christ. The average amount
of time for this deeper conversion, on campus, has
been roughly six to 18 months. The timeframe can
be shortened when we meet someone who has already encountered Jesus and who only needs a little
help figuring out how to follow him. If they are ready
to serve, they can begin to love, care for, and lead
others more quickly because our work with them
does not end when they begin to care for others. This
is critical.

The Impact

As I stated earlier, in FOCUS we use the terms "win, build, send" to represent Encounter, Accompaniment, and Spirit-Filled Evangelizers. It is critical to note that winning and building do not end when someone has been sent to win, build, and send others. It takes years to mature in Christ, and in reality, we never stop.

For example, I once worked with a young man named John. At the time, John had a recent conversion back to his Catholic faith. He knew the basics, but he was still very young in his faith. I began to mentor him and teach him how to read the Scriptures. I invited him to join me in daily prayer and Mass. He spent time with my wife and family and learned by example what it meant to live a life dedicated to Jesus and his mission. Just a month or so after we began, John began work with two different groups of men in two different cities. John did not know too much, but he knew the truths I had taught and modeled for him over a few weeks and he began to share those truths with the men he was working with. He began to invest his life in these men, and as a result, transformation began to take place.

Soon, the men with whom John was working were themselves working with other men. Over the next few years, hundreds of lives were impacted. From those first two groups, at least four men became priests, others became missionaries, and still others became Spirit-filled evangelists and multipliers who are now living lives in parishes and raising families. Since then, John has matured. The basic Christian teaching I taught John has all been well covered; in fact, John has gone on to receive a master's degree in theology. John speaks all over the country and teaches people about the faith, helping them to see the vision for becoming missionary disciples themselves. More importantly, John continues to invest deeply in a few and cultivate faithfulness and fruitfulness.

John's story is amazing, but it does not stand alone. John is just one of the more than 1,000 FOCUS missionaries who have practiced "win, build, send"—helping people to encounter Jesus, accompanying them by investing in a few and sharing not only the gospel of God but their very selves, and sending them out to become Spirit-filled evangelists and multipliers. Thousands of students who never became full-time missionaries have walked the same path, living joy-filled lives and teaching others how to do the same.

* * *

I trust that, if you have read this far, you have a desire to see your parish, your apostolate, or your family radiate a culture of missionary discipleship. We have looked at three habits that ensure our efforts will bear fruit and a three-phased Method Modeled by the Master, which offer a pathway for transforming the culture and even the world. If this is where you want to go and how you would like to get there, we are happy to help. We have materials in written, audio, and video formats available at no cost, which we utilize in training our staff and student leaders. They are available to you here:

<u>www.focus.org</u>
<u>www.focusoncampus.org/resources</u>

In Gratitude

To those I have been blessed to walk with: my wife and soul-mate, Michaelann, and my parents, Brock and Carole. To Roy, Scott, and Jim, who walked me back to Christ; to Leon, Eric, Mike, Paul, and Ron, who walked with me as I came back to the Church; and to Scott, Tim, Sean, James, and Ted, for our times of study. Finally, in the work of FOCUS, to Archbishop Charles, Craig, John, Matthew, Fr. John, Mark, Sam, Hilary, and Brock. I pray there will be many more, a few at a time…

Curtis Martin
Founder of FOCUS